The Secret to your Chakra's

Tammy Adams

ISBN: 0692511830
ISBN-13: 9780692511831

DEDICATION

I give thanks to God and our Angels for giving me the connection I am so blessed to have.

I thank my husband, Jim Adams, for the support and the love he has always given me. Without him I would not be here today. I give thanks for my four children who have brought tears of joy and sadness because without them I would not have learned patience.

I am thankful for the parents I chose in this lifetime. For without them I surely would not have had the experiences I had to make me who I am today.

CONTENTS

ACKNOWLEDGMENTS

I want to give acknowledgment to the House of Angels Foundation, 501©3. The House of Angels Foundation has made it possible for me to write this book to provide everyone with this knowledge. This book is giving all of you the information you need so you can continue to grow, become reconnected, and live a balanced life once again. The Foundation is a nonprofit which helps people become reconnected to wellness and spiritual awakening around the world. It is a nondenominational spiritual nonprofit organization that is helping to create awakening, self-awareness, and self-love.

The House of Angels Foundation has been around since 2004 and has been helping people in many ways around the world. Now, I am thankful that they are helping me to create a global movement with, "The Secret to your Chakra." All of the proceeds from the sale of this book will go to the Foundation so that it can continue to grow around the world and help people in all the ways they need.

I hope this book brings you the gifts you all need individually to continue to grow and be the perfect you, God bless.

Tammy Adams

Introduction

In the beginning, we were all energy and we had no form. Today, things have changed quite a bit, we are much more complex than "day one" of our universe.

What is energy and what are chakras?

This book is all about teaching you how to understand energy and the aura around us. We get confused because there are so many mixed messages out there, so this is what drove me to write this book. I wanted to help the people I work with understand chakra energy—which is always available to us.

I want to see all people aligned and no longer in a fog or covered in dark spots. What this means is we are letting ourselves get disconnected from the original, one source and we are moving farther and farther away from the real truth; we are becoming more desensitized.

Is this the way you want our future to be? Well, I don't, and I want to wake up in the morning and see a rainbow of colors surrounding people instead of dark spots or splashes of grey. We are filled with different energies, of which I will give simple short explanations within this book.

We are like a rainbow of color and this is what I see when I look at someone who is aligned. An aligned person has a rainbow surrounding him or her. We have seven energy points and levels in our body that are what we call chakras. We are made of different colors representing different energies. I am not always sure how we have allowed ourselves to get so detached, but we have and sometimes become very distant from our original creation, which was perfect in itself.

In the beginning, we all were aware of our surroundings. We had a connection to the life around us; i.e., the trees, the sun, the water, the moon, the plants, the soil, and the animals. There was no disconnection and we felt what was around us. We did not just see it. Now we let ourselves walk around ignoring the fact that there is something majorly wrong with the planet that we call home.

What lead me to writing this book was that I see the sadness in people and the blank look on people faces whenever I explain what chakras are; I find people many are blocked. That's is why I wrote a book to help all of you get back on track and in balance. Dreams do come true and we can once again become whole and be reconnected. Have faith and trust that our angels and messengers, such as myself, are here to guide you and show you the way.

In this book you will go through a roller coaster of emotions. I won't say this will be easy. I do advise to go through this carefully and pay full attention. This book has been created to help get you from point a to point z in a flash without all the confusion. I will make it easy like those books for "dummies"—which you are not—so that you will get the points, the messages, and together, we get to the solution!

I have been told by the angels that this is needed, as well as many other books I am writing, which are soon to follow. All of these books will help those who just need a quick reference or a quick guide of information, so keep your eyes open to see the truth. The new books will follow shortly after this one, and will be available to people working with me, and the rest of the world. That is my vision.

First Chakra

WELCOME TO, "The Secret to your Chakra," a hand-held book you can carry around for the benefit of helping change the energies that have been blocked within. I have been around the world working, helping, and teaching people just like you how to open your chakras so that you can have balance in all that you do.

So that you may never feel as though you are alone on this path, you can talk to your own angel who is beside you right now as we speak. Your angel will then be able to share visions with you more clearly and you will no longer be wondering if what you see is real. You will know the truth

God has created a perfect way for us to remain connected and have balance within our lives, but as we are all well aware, the way things go can cause us to become disconnected from the source. Why? Well the answer is easy. We become way too busy dealing with work, social life, money, family drama, kids, plus much more. We have so many things that side track us away from where we should be.

I am here to share with you a very short manual about how to get back on track and get balanced.

Consider my book a handbook you can keep in your briefcase, in your purse or even in the armrest of your car. I believe having it available and easy to read will help you get just the basics that you need to understand in a way that you can actually apply the teachings I am giving you.

Keeping it simple, we have seven energy points and levels in our bodies. These energy points are called chakras; these chakras are what makes/creates the Aura around us. Some people may think that chakras are a little hokey, but the truth is we have been surrounded by Auras throughout our lives and I will explain.

First off, many people say that they do not believe that chakras actually have power to them, that they do not consist of energy and it is all in the mind. That we make things up or we wish it to come true. I say yes, we can create our own destiny and yes, we can do so by visualizing a situation we desire and bring that energy towards us. This is called the power of the universe and is a whole other book.

What I am here to teach you is about the chakras and how we have had them around us all the time. Even those people who believe only in science and not angels or a God have them. Well, surprise to all of you is that the southern lights and the northern lights are called (Aurora Borealis). The word Aura has been right there in front of all of us for many years and yet many of us still do not realize this. The reason for this is they say that the lights around the southern and northern tips of our planet are just created from gases. The truth is that the pictures we have all seen and that many scientists have studied are of the aura and energy of the planet.

The point is, the aura is real, it is alive, and is huge part of the reason why you are the way you are. Thus, I am here to help and teach you how to heal and open your chakras so that you may finally be realigned and in balance.

Root Chakra

The first chakra is called the Root Chakra. Now, when you hear the word "root" what automatically comes to your mind?

To me, I instantly think of a foundation, which without it, we would surely fall and be off balance for sure. This is true, for without your foundation being correct, open and in balance— or even facing an opposite direction—you can have a lot of difficulties!

Chakras can be shut off in many ways. It's not hard to imagine that most of the time the first chakra is usually shut off due to fear or pain from childhood. The root chakra has to do with family issues or even relationship issues. Why do we hold on to these issues? Ask yourself why you want to own them instead of letting them go and allowing these blockages to be washed away? Let them heal so that you can grow and prosper in life rather than having a feeling of standing still.

Having the first chakra out of balance, I feel, is really detrimental. In order for us to be in balance, it's easy to understand when we realize it's the root and the foundation of you. All foundations in life need to be in balance, without which we may tilt, fall, or no longer grow upright.

The first chakra is for the grounding of one's self; it is for strength and confidence as well. When you are standing tall, you can see clearly, you can feel confident. But if you are tilting or in reverse facing the wrong way you may feel limp or lack of confidence.

There are many ways to block the Root Chakra but the most important thing you need to know about this one is that you can heal it and bring it to be your core, once again becoming your strength and your power.

The root chakra is located at your tailbone, right at the very tip of your spine. So, if you are working on clearing this chakra the best thing to do would be to surround this area in red (the color of blood) to get the flow of life back into it and get the energy pumping and pushing up through the rest of your body.

In order for it to reach the very top of your seventh chakra known as the Crown you need to have the Root Chakra be very strong and stable. See the red being forced up through your spine up to the very top of your head and see the red then spread out throughout your fingertips and your toes. You want the red to cover your whole being, your whole body.

The best way to do this is going into a meditation. There are several ways to meditate; one is lying down on a flat surface on your back. Always remember that no matter where you meditate or how you do it, never wear metal. Metal blocks the energy flow and stops us from connecting to our own energy, which is the whole purpose of this. Connecting to your own energy is a feeling I cannot say with words. You need to just go through the steps. I will guide you through and you will see for yourself. Everyone is different, and each person will have a different result, so do not think we are all the same. This is not true.

Instructions to Balance Root Chakra

You can lie down on a flat surface on you back with no metal and no shoes is best; or you can sit in the lotus position, which is best for the seventh chakra so for the first chakra, to be honest, I would recommend lying down flat. Or you can even go for a walk or go to the mountains and/or go by the water. Whatever way you choose to do this is all up to you. Remember that nature is always a good place to be when you are trying to heal anything, because nature is all about giving and healing. Know this: giving back to nature just by being thankful or helping clean her up is also a good thing.

So, when you decide the way you choose to mediate for twenty minutes, you will be focusing on each one of the colors I will explain in the rest of the chapters which are the colors of the other chakras. During this meditation you will feel things; always keep a journal of what you are feeling, seeing or going through, so that you can see your progress and the movement that is happening within you.

Follow the color in each chapter to see it so that you can let if flow through you as it is meant to flow.

For the Root Chakra, you want the red to flow very powerfully from the bottom of your spine to the top of your head. Let it then move throughout your body to reach your fingertips and toes. Here you will see many sad thoughts and you may even feel a bit of pain in this chakra because it is such a grounding one; it carries a lot of weight, stress, worry, and blockages.

I find that people with this blockage do not have good relationships, so you may also see this in your life. If so, you can change it!

You may also have complications with your lower back because the chakras can be tricky and can trick us into thinking we are ill with medical problems. But, the truth is many of us are not ill at all; we just are blocked and not even doctors can find the solutions because the blockages have nothing to do with an illness. The bad news is that if we continue ignoring the blockages, then eventually we can create a health problem in each chakra because our energy reflects in our bodies. For us not to know this is ignorance. To be honest, we all need to know that what we do to ourselves even emotionally can create and have a huge effect on our lives, bodies, and energy.

Use this handbook to help teach yourself how to heal and release some of the pressure you may have in your energy field. By all means let it get started and do it well. Remember this is neither a race nor a test. It's just you taking it one step at a time for healing yourself.

Write also in your journal about the dreams you may have during this process as they often have messages from our angels to help guide us a bit more.

God Bless!

Second Chakra

HERE, WE ARE at an important chakra! Yes, they are all important, but without this one, your creativity and freedom will be blocked—the freedom and willingness to be who you really are! I have noticed the second chakra quite often does not get a lot of attention in the right way, so hopefully I can help you understand it and get you in balance quick and easy.

The second chakra is all about passion, love, intimacy, creativity, and openness. Here you will be able to see who you are and find yourself with this one, because it is where your passion for life comes through. So many people emphasize that this chakra is only about sex, but this is not true. Yes, it is about passion and yes, it's about intimacy and love, but it's much more than that.

Called the Sacral Chakra, it is located right at your pelvis, is beneficial in so many ways regarding creativity. Without passion you cannot have creativity. So, this one is for those who are looking for guidance and is for those who may feel like they are boring or both.

Do you believe you know what you want to do in life? Do you feel as though you know who you are? Well this chakra is the one that will help you see who you are and find out what your passion is. Many of us lose our passion because we are taught from a young age that we are meant to be logical and not free to be who we want to be.

The sad thing is I see and hear this all the time, and yet we say we need artists, we need people to care for the planet, and we need people to bring forth their passion. Well, the Sacral Chakra is where the passion comes from. If you want to learn how to live life fully and no longer just exist, this is the place where it will explode, and you will finally be free.

What are your dreams? What do you remember when you were a young child fantasizing about being "something" when you grew up? So, what are you doing now and what are you working on becoming as in your dream career and living your purpose? What are the things you remember that have held you back? Who was it that stopped you from being who you are meant to be? And why did this person do that?

Well, here is an important part. I need you to forgive them, so you can heal and let go of the past—to let go of that pain. Many of us do not even know we are blocked. I have worked with so many people saying they have worked really hard on being in balance, but they had several blocks. Their chakras were backwards not just sometimes blocked; it as though I am looking at a zigzag line where you are supposed to be a straight line. There are so many things to teach all of you, but I have to make sure to just teach the very basics to help you get in balance and just get the points.

So, figure out whoever caused you this "held-back" feeling; go deep within because only you can find this out. Some people who cannot see into their childhood or just carry too much pain, can try another solution and go to someone who can see it; someone who can talk to your angel, so your angel can give you the answer you need to help you remember what had happened way back when.

During this process you don't want to "fake" your movement. By this I mean becoming honest with yourself, truly looking in the mirror and asking yourself: Who am I? Who do I want to be? What do I want out of life? Then watch as the doors open within you.

Sacral Chakra

The Sacral Chakra is a hard one because it's about emotion and passion. As I said, we are taught to push it away or hold back from who we want to be; we are even shown in school that we need to be logical—not creative, not free. But those who are completely connected and open with this chakra are world famous in some way because they had the confidence, the passion, and did not let one thing hold them back or down.

I say we are *all* meant to live free and at the top of the world! I have heard some people say that there is meant to be a balance in life with a portion of worker bees and queen bees that keep the hive alive. Usually there are many more worker bees than there are queens. Now, in regards towards bees perhaps this is true, but we are not talking about bees we are talking about people. And we as humans have the potential to be anything we want to be. If we have the ability to go to outer space, and the ability to go to the depths of the sea, then why not imagine you can fly? Go for it, stop holding yourself back, start to open your eyes and become alive and let yourself live.

We have so many things that need repair on this planet and maybe that's your purpose? We need more healers and maybe that's your purpose? But you may never know what your purpose is unless you open up to your sacral chakra and see and feel the passion.

As to sex issues, if your sacral chakra is blocked you may not be able to perform well during intimacy or you'll feel as though you are not turned on. You may be carrying fear. If you were abused sexually you will surely be blocked here unless you have already healed this in your past.

You can have blocks if you have not been with the right partner and you feel as though you have been just a bed slave of some sort. If you are not getting any type of satisfaction out of the sexual experience, you are not open. This chakra is for pleasure and without the pleasure of your own intimacy, you are not being free. You may come up with many reasons why this pleasure is not needed, but they will all lead back to "yes" you do. When God created us, women were designed to bare children. We were also given the desire to be touched by a man or a man being touched by a woman. It's the way creation planted these intimacy cycles within our whole beings.

Denying yourself of intimacy is a very heavy block you may not want to be facing. Being free with your feeling of how you want to be touched is a must just as much as being connected to how you do *not* want to be touched.

The Color Orange

The point is to open your chakra and let yourself be free and not for the sake of others but for the sake of yourself. To allow your passion, your creativity be wild and open. Let the color orange fill your pelvis and let it come in through your belly button. The color orange is meant to bring forth warmth and friendship with yourself; you want the orange to fill up inside of you and cover your lower stomach area first.

This will start to feel as though you are getting a pressure and warmth surrounding this area of the sacral location but keep going until you are finished meditating 20 minutes at least. At the end of the meditation, remember to write down what you felt and what you saw; this part is important to see the results, so you can continue growing. Know this: you *cannot* be healed in just 20 minutes; this is an ongoing process because this area of your body has been stuck for so long and you need to work it slowly and get it to move like an unclogged pipe.

You will know this is blocked if you feel pain in your pelvis or if you have issues with your uterus or prostate. You will feel as though you have health issues or pain. These are warnings that your energy field is blocked, but most of the time you are not blocked health-wise, thank God—it is just a warning unless you ignore it until it becomes a more serious problem.

Good luck! This one is deep.

God Bless!

Third Chakra

WELCOME TO THE third chakra, the Solar Plexus. Here is where many of your beliefs, your guidance, and your true gut feelings come from.   This chakra is located in the upper part of your stomach and is a powerful chakra. It's in combination with the third eye; these two almost work together but are very separate.

The location is important to remember because many people do not realize that it goes back to what we've heard for thousands of years: "listen to your gut it will guide you," or another saying, "if you want to know which way to turn pay attention to your sixth sense feeling." I could go on and on, but I'd rather teach you than repeat sayings; just wanted to mention a few so you recognize them as common sentiments throughout your lifetime.

Many people try to ignore that chakras are real or that they are important, however, we have used them throughout the years while never even giving them credit where the credit is due. Chakras have been called so many different things for a long time except the right name "chakras." Why are we so afraid to say what they really are? Because if we do allow ourselves to pay attention and give them credit or recognize them, it means we need to change. Oh boy, that word again change!

Why is change so bad? Everything is great about changing. I feel it is what makes the world go around, and yet some things are meant to be left unchanged such as the knowledge about chakras and how to use them. So, this is why I'm here to teach you and show you how to use them properly and effectively to have wonderful results. We are all connected in a way, but we insist on doing whatever we can to disconnect and go off on our own.

God has created us to be as a unity. I cannot say this enough because many of us are saying in our heads, "but then how do we become an individual?" Well I can help you with that but understand this: being an individual has nothing to do with being alone and disconnected from the main source that we all feed off—the energy that was created since the beginning.

God is the source, the light and that energy. Many people have come up with other names or titles for God and that is a great, wonderful thing to have your very own connection and your very own name for God. Even as a child, I asked these questions: what is God, who is God? Then I saw for myself through a personal experience that I was so honored to have gone through: God is all, and is everywhere and everything—light, energy, wind, shapes, and water plus much more. So, let yourself know that during your process of opening up the chakras from the first to the seventh, that connection is the key to it all.

Knowing the information properly is important to me so that people will be in balance and reconnected to themselves and not giving their power away. So, the third chakra is all about your power, your abilities, and your gift. Use your abilities to benefit you and your life so that doors can open, and you can be walking the proper path.

Solar Plexus Chakra

The third chakra is called the Solar Plexus, which is where your intuition comes from like I mentioned earlier (our gut feeling). It's really the intuitive abilities that were given to us to help ourselves at the time of conception. It's a way for us to connect to our own path, purpose, and a way to protect us from being misled. How we do this is by paying attention to the energy that flows throughout our bodies and feel what direction our angel is guiding us towards. You can allow your Solar Plexus to guide you.

The Solar Plexus is your inner voice; it is the guidance from your angels. How do we use it to our benefit? Well one thing I teach is pay attention daily to the energy that flows through you, what you are feeling about whatever you need to do, go left go right or go straight. Use your intuition it's a gift we all were given to help us individually.

If your Solar Plexus is blocked, how would you know? Well it is clear your ability to follow your intuition could fail and perhaps you might feel as though you are dizzy. There are many ways we can feel disconnected, but when it comes to this chakra I believe it is so beneficial to have this one open. If it's not open, you may feel as though you're very indecisive when it comes to making choices. You may feel some blockages in your upper stomach this is another clear sign. Your intestines are connected to this chakra.

The Color Yellow

Best way to heal the Solar Plexus and get it open once again is to go through a healing of the place where it started and see when you first started closing yourself off from using your own natural gifts. Also, you need to use the color yellow to send peace and healing to this chakra.

See the color yellow surrounding your Solar Plexus at the center of the chakra then visualize it coming all the way out until it has filled your upper stomach area. You do not need it to fill your whole body; if you want to, by all means do so, then continue and let the color yellow surround the whole body. But this may a be a little hard so keep this up until you see the movement and feel it as well.

Also, you will feel your intuition working all a of the sudden and giving you great clear direction. You will feel clear and guided, not confused or lost.

God Bless!

Fourth Chakra

THE FOURTH CHAKRA is the heart felt one and is so important in life! You cannot smile or be happy without this one being in balance. Your fourth chakra is the Heart Chakra; this is the one that will help you in love.

Many people do not understand that having balance in life is so necessary. We think we can survive without having it. Well, we can survive but we will not be healthy. People often think they know what's best because they are the ones living their own lives. Yes, I agree it is *your* life and you may think you know what is best—especially, if your third chakra (intuition and gut instinct) is not blocked. But to be honest, in working with many people, I see one thing a lot of people try to do. They do everything they can to take a short cut—even I have tried it! I get it life has a lot of things to handle everyday: family, work, bills, and then emotion. Yes, it may be hard sometimes and it may even be hurtful, but love is a huge part of life.

We get hurt and close ourselves off from love because other people in our past may have given us some bad examples of love. Our angels want us to be happy as they give us love, teach us love and want us to share love every day. However, we sometimes think in our own minds, for some ingrained irrational reason, that it is okay to live without love. That we can survive the loneliness and just make up for it by working even harder and ignoring we need love to thrive.

Do you actually think that when you are at the end of your life you will go back to your bank account and say, "baby I love you?" And then your money is going to respond back by keeping you warm with hugs and snuggles or maybe go get you a blanket if you're cold and walk to get you a glass of water if you are thirsty. No way!

I have heard so many stories and I am sure I have not heard them all, as new things happen each day. But I assure you they are not much different than the ones I have already worked with for the last few decades. I have been teaching and personally working with people one on one with their energy, or talking with their angels, and I assure you that if you do not have love, you are not fulfilled in life.

Yes, there are those occasions where you could have had your true love, but your better half might have left this earthly plane and you are waiting to reunite once again through the pearly golden gates of heaven. But this is not who I am reaching out to. I call out to those who may be putting their heads down with worry and fear, with doubt or disgust, in just the thought of wanting to have true love.

The truth is that love is what makes the world go around. Without it, how would we survive as a species? We would surely wither away. Without true love we would have no heartfelt people wanting to change our planet into a better place. Our home, which we call earth, would then have much more neglect and we don't want that. Love is much more than we give it credit for.

What do you think people die from? Broken hearts that's what. What about when you see someone who was in love and whose soulmate dies? Even when the other half is still alive, if they were so connected on a high vibration between them, we often see the other half die shortly thereafter.

Heart Chakra

The Heart Chakra is located at the center of your chest right in the middle of the rib cage not at the location of your real heart to the left. It is in the center. Remember chakras are aligned in a straight line from top to bottom starting at your tailbone to the very top of your head.

What do you want to do now after hearing the information you have learned today?

Well, let me continue on to this track. If you are blocked in any chakra, your health will start to also fail in your arteries and even the heart will have complications. I don't care how healthy you think you are, this has nothing to do with your diet intake, your workout schedule, or your blood pressure, etc.

Many people try to blame so many things for their poor health problems that are heart related and do not give credit due where it should be given. Yes, our Heart Chakra can cause a large amount of health problems, these are the ones you can die from because most people ignore this subject to play it safe. Or we try to say it is out of protection from getting hurt again. When your heart is neglected and closed off energetically, it makes us feel physical pain from this blockage. And, this result can show up in a number of ailments.

The Color of Green

How do you heal this one? Well, first of all the color for this one is green, which is so significant. I feel like green is about healing and it also is the color to bring forward success. So funny it would be the one to heal our hearts. When you think of your heart and how to heal it, many of us would go straight to the color red—the color of Valentines—but this is not true.

Green is the color you need to see in the center of your rib cage and let this color go from the center of this chakra and then cover the body slowly. This one you want to move slowly; do not rush this process because you do not want to leave anything out.

What I mean by this is as you are focusing on the color green and visualizing this color in your heart chakra, then you see the people who may have been the ones to create the blockages: see these people whether it's a parent, a teacher, a stranger, or even someone who has abused you. See this person and forgive this person or persons. It is a must. You cannot heal unless you heal the pain. If you do not forgive them, you are cheating the process of healing correctly and many people do this (they CHEAT themselves).

I do things the right way. I show you how to do it correctly, so if this is what you want then this is what you do. I know what I am saying is very hard; it's not easy. I know this, but this is why you do this slowly. Slow and steady always wins in the end. Remember this is not a race to the finish line. There is no race, so if you share this book or you give the information to someone you care for, make sure you know not try to do this as a competition. Take your time and do this right.

Breathe in love and exhale the pain of the sadness and the worry. Let your heart feel worthy of love and the chakra will slowly open and you will feel so light and so uplifted like love is surrounding you. Not love in an intimate way; I mean love in a caring gentle way towards people and the planet—and above all, loving yourself! Your thoughts will change, and your reactions will change, which is the great part of all this work!

God Bless!

Fifth Chakra

WELL, WE ARE doing great and working our way up, yeah! By now you should be so proud and feeling much better.

Throat Chakra

This is the Throat Chakra, which is an easy one; a really clear one at your throat. I laugh because the other chakras are so much more detail to me, but this one is very clear—right in the center of your throat of course—and without a doubt you should be able to feel this one if it's blocked.

Most people notice this one right away. First off you may feel as though you have a lump in your throat. We often think the reason we have these feelings in our physical body means we are sick, or something is wrong. You got that right! Yes, there is something wrong, but it is quite often not something you can fix medically. Actually, the truth about most health problems is that doctors don't find the solution because it was not a medical issue in the first place.

I have a few different doctors who are my clients, and they send me referrals all the time because they understand firsthand how it works after the results they have received from working with me. I teach people how to heal themselves, which is how someone can tell the difference between a true illness and just a blocked chakra.

It may sound a little farfetched, but I am telling you a true fact here. Our chakras have much more power than we realize and it's time we start listening to them, so we can finally get ahead and be on top of all these energy points and levels within our bodies. Live and be happy to the fullest and feel great. How do you like this vision? My hope is that what I just wrote will sink in. That you let it hit home, so you remain inspired to continue plugging away at what needs to be done to get you completely balanced.

We have so many reasons why we don't do the work we need to do, and our throat chakra is a perfect place to talk about this. Our throats are about communication. We are taught since childhood to mind others and behave. Well, we have been told the wrong thing since day one. We are really here to speak our minds and express our deepest desires or dreams.

So, why is it that just a few numbers of people on this planet can do that and succeed? Well, I will tell you why; because something within them would not let them give up or be told to be quiet and just sit in the back. Their angels, or maybe even rarely at times a human will give this guidance, like I have with my children.

Those people who stepped up and said what was on their minds and spoke up to express their dreams were examples for all of us; these include Martin Luther King Jr., John F. Kennedy, Mother Teresa, and of course my favorite, Jesus.

There are others as well, but I wanted to get your attention with the ones that the world knows who have made a difference. And yes, maybe Jesus had a whole choir of angels along with an army, but still he did speak up.

We think just because we are told to shut off our thoughts and our desires, we should really do this. No, No, No! We need to speak up and say what we feel and say what we want out of life. Our throat chakra is all about getting us where we are meant to be through expression. Our whole purpose is about being outspoken and getting to where we want to be in life; it is not about standing still. I know life does not come to us. We need to follow life and go to it. We cannot wait by our doors—it's just not that way.

Our throats get blocked by not using them. They get filled with fear and concern about other people's' opinions (what will this person think of me if I say what I feel?). This is no way to live. I know if you have the love and faith in yourself like it was meant to be since day one, I promise you success is not far behind.

Expression is how we get what we want. Otherwise, it will never happen. Open your eyes to see your life and see what you are surrounded by, and ask yourself this very simple question: "AM I HAPPY?"

Don't be logical or analytical to get your answer, but just be free and answer freely. You will then see where you are being held back. I want more than anything for us to live on a peaceful amazing planet and be free and live clean. This small dream can come true by following your voice.

The Color Blue

You need to want to help yourself—you cannot fake this. So first off, look for the color blue when you close your eyes. Remember each meditation is very similar: laying down flat or sitting in the lotus position depending on what you prefer. Then close your eyes, breathe in blue light, like a light sky-blue color, not dark blue. What you want is to feel your breath coming out through your throat and feel it then coming in through your throat. You will see all the denial or the failure you may have had being washed away. See disappointments as success stories as to how you can do better. Look at the bigger picture of who you can be.

Inhale the positive and exhale the stuff you no longer want to own or be a part of and let go of the things that have made you sad or upset. Let all the dark energy flow out and keep breathing in the light. Let this light fill your whole body as if it is water going down your throat then spreading out to give your body the water it needs to keep it alive.

Let the energy fill you and then the best thing to do is return to your journal of what you feel during these meditations. Journal so you can keep track of your success and work in progress. Later, you can look back and see how you have grown and just maybe then, you can be happy and fulfilled.

Life is so wonderful! Let this experience of going through this book fill you with inspiration to get yourself to places you never knew were even an opportunity. Allow yourself to see that truly anything is possible and use your voice and use the gift of sounds that God gave you. Your angels are right there so let them help you.

Not only will you be happy, but you will also feel healthier and more alive.

God Bless!

Sixth Chakra

HERE IS WHERE things really begin to become so clear for you and you will no longer feel foggy. This is the sixth chakra, and it is located where the center of your eyebrows is and a little above them. It is right in the middle of your forehead.

Many people think that this is the only chakra that has to do with intuition, but this is not true because if you recall, the Solar Plexus is also about intuition just at another level. We have so many blessings. I believe it is because of all these energy points and levels within us are to help us in all areas of our life and show us the way we need to go. We are *never* left unaided.

I teach people how to connect to each one of these chakras so that they can have complete movement as it is meant to be. Our angels are always nearby but sometimes we forget to listen. Do we pay attention to the messages or even the signs? Ask yourself when was the last time you let yourself follow the path your angel told you?

What was the last thing you remember being told? Write down the messages; I always advise this. Pay attention once you are clear and keep yourself moving forward and moving up with your purpose.

The Third Eye

The sixth chakra is called the third eye because it is literally where your third eye is located. We are all born with a gift to see the path we are meant to be upon. We are gifted with vision to see just a few steps ahead in our lives. We also are given this gift to warn us and protect us from any harm. We are told when to turn and when to stop so that we can avoid mistakes.

Our third eye is such a powerful chakra it is meant to show us visions of things we did not think were even possible. I know so many people, that once I helped them open this chakra they were then able to have great success in many areas of their lives.

You can use this chakra to guide you in all subjects not just certain things. You can see anything through the Third Eye. It is for vision, for intuition, and it is where our psychic ability comes from.

Can you identify some feelings you have felt in your life from this chakra? I am sure one of them is a sense of déjà vu. This term has often been used to express intuition. But sometimes people think that we're saying we are psychic or having a vision means we are weird or having a possession from the dark side. A lot of people do not realize that the sixth chakra is totally for our benefit. We are so fortunate to have such a gift, but we toss it away out of fear and not being certain about what others may say or think. There is no way darkness can be talking to us or giving us déjà vu if the information is most of the time always a good message.

Very rarely will you get a message that is not so good. I am even a victim of people expressing that maybe I'm talking to something else besides angels. Then I respond by saying exactly this:

"God has given us angels since day one, so how could it be a bad thing if every prophet ever mentioned has talked with angels?"

I know that people say many things when it comes to this subject, just as there are many ways we can disconnect from this chakra by allowing it to get closed; it's common to see this chakra closed. It is not good, but it is true. Why do we let people get in the way of our personal relationship with our angels?

God thought of everything and created us in such a way so that we are able to protect ourselves. How amazing is that? When I sit back and think about it. I still get amazed because we do not realize how much thought and love was put into creating us and giving us life.

We sometimes get caught up in "The Big Bang Theory," and that maybe we were created by the stars colliding. Well, how could this be possible when just the simple knowledge of seeing how we are created with our right side being exactly the same as our left side. And such a complicated yet perfect design of our insides, is undeniable proof that we are part of a *creation* not just a big bang.

There is a simple sign to show you when this chakra is closed off. Your brain will feel foggy as though you are having a tug of war within you. Your head will feel heavy maybe or you can also have difficulties with headaches if you are really blocked.

Why it is not good to have this chakra blocked is because we need to know what our direction should be. Yes, somethings are meant to be a mystery, I agree. But it is not like our abilities are going to tell us everything. Instead, it is for warning and for guidance. Our psychic ability is for our total benefit.

The Color Purple

If the Third Eye is blocked, we will not have a knowing and we will feel as though we are a bit lost. What we need to do to have healing is focus on the color purple and breathe in the color and let yourself feel it fill you from head to toe, letting your mind go clear.

Many people do not think it is important to have the sixth chakra open, but I believe that this is a necessary one for you. So, we'll be doing the exercises to open this chakra and create clarity and a knowing that what you feel is all that matters! Do not pay attention to others. Let your opinion be the one that matters and just listen to the advice from others if it will help you in a positive manner.

When breathing in the purple, focus on seeing your mind open up, as though there is a huge door that is now slowly cracking open until the bright purple light shines through to cover you in this color. Purple has always been an intuition color so this one is perfect for what you are working on in the Third Eye.

See the energy go within your soul not just your body and mind. This one you want to go deep to the core so that your connection to your angel will be very strong and powerful. You want to radiate light and be the example everyone wants to be like. Be the one now and let yourself shine. Make sure you cover yourself every day in a ball of clear light that is a shield of protection.

Protection is even for those at a high level who know a lot or even for those who already feel protected. They still need to continue this daily routine so that when caught off guard, they are protected with this light that only lets good energy into our field and nothing can break it.

God Bless!

Seventh Chakra

WOW! YOU MADE it to the final chakra. Congratulations, it's a big one.

Most people do not even pay attention to the seventh chakra until the end of their days. This one is very powerful and has the most significance. This chakra is all about God, all about our connection to the higher self. It is for those who are here as guides, mentors and healers.

This chakra is about love and passion and is for those seeking truth and knowledge. Of course, I love this one. It may be my favorite because its purpose is to keep your connection to God, a straight line with no interference. Many of us do not have this one open because we are so involved in the world and the rat race of going through the motions in life rather than actually living life and enjoying the gift of it.

Life is so filled with adventure. Sadly, we often let the adventures pass us right by. Then, sometime near the end of our days in this life, we open our eyes and look at the things we have done, what we accomplished, and what we left behind for others to gain from.

Our angels talk to us daily giving us guidance, messages, and dreams but what do we do? We overlook them or over analyze them. "What is this really about?" You may be asking yourself right now. Well, it is about me suggesting to you to not wait till the end of your days here on earth; use your seventh chakra now and get the benefit of knowing how to love life.

We are a very blessed species. I have seen how many times we have been lifted and saved from our very own disasters that we could have created in our lives. Today as you go through these chakras step by step let yourself open this very last one to help you have the light fill you and your soul from inside out.

A soul connection is much better than just a body connection. If you want to know who God is, you can see and get to know God here with this chakra. It is a wonderful gift we are given once again.

Do not hesitate to let yourself reach out and take what you want so that your soul, your body, and your mind can have true fulfillment and completion. I love when we connect to our brightest light because this is where any fear you ever thought about starts to fade away until it has been completely surrounded by the love and light of pure energy from God.

Crown Chakra

This chakra is called the Crown Chakra because this is where we are being crowned and connecting on a completely different level.

I know people who have expressed feelings of tingles at the location of where their crown chakra is. This means that there is communication from your angel, so it's a good idea to pay attention and really hear what it is your angel is trying to tell you.

What is the Crown Chakra? It is the location where you connect with God and your angel; it is the location of true connection and where it all happens on a deeper, more spiritual level. This is where you finally reach a level of completion a feeling that you are there. Like I said, many people do not open this until they are passing and at that time they start to talk to their angel and even passed loved ones very clearly. We can even see it with our own eyes.

In one example, I was recently speaking to a woman who told me her mother never believed we can talk to angels or talk to the dead. Well, at that time, her mother was ill and in the process of passing. She had just a few days left to say her goodbyes and come to peace about her passing. All of a sudden, her mother starts talking out loud to her late husband and her angel—she actually saw a few angels with her in the room. Now the daughter, who was with the mother the whole time during her last moments/days, saw nothing. No angel, nor her father, but she was witnessing her mother talking to them as if they were right there sitting down in the room on the chair beside her.

It is real everyone! We can talk to our loved ones who have passed away and this is the chakra that makes it all happen. If you're ready to have this chakra open, I promise you it will be mind-blowing; you will witness things you never knew were possible. I am sure of this.

It is not scary. Most people do not want this chakra open out of fear of seeing the other side and being freaked out or startled somehow. I have only had people thank me and be so happy after I have opened this chakra for them.

This is the place where you will have enlightenment, understanding and a lot of the questions answered you have had in life (Can we talk to angels? Is God able to speak with us?). You get this download of knowledge all of a sudden and then you are able to see things in a way you never saw them before.

Life is a gift, a fun, exciting adventure, and we are given such wonderful tools to have and use so that we can experience only success in our lives. Our chakras are the tools that lead us, guide us, and warn us through all subjects in our lives. There is surely nothing left out when it comes to us having the right chakra for the right situation.

The Color Pink

To use the crown chakra, you need to visualize pink; this is the color for the crown, which is the color for love, for soft passionate energy. I love the way the color wheel works when it comes to the chakras because they are not as we think they should be. Such as the pink or red for the heart, instead the heart is green. It's so perfect for the crown to see this pink as a pastel, not a strong hot pink color. You always want to start off with soft colors so this way you are able to work your way up to the more powerful energy when you are ready for it.

To reach results for this one, being in the lotus position is best. The reason is you want the energy going up towards the sky, which doesn't work well by lying down. Lying down will defeat the connection with God and the angels; you want the energy to flow up—not any other direction.

See this color in your Crown Chakra as though you have a halo around you. This is a great way to form the energy to the Crown Chakra. Then have the color be as though they are small raindrops falling into you until you become filled from head to toe with pink color. Your energy will feel like you are floating.

Use this feeling to carry you through tough times or even just enjoy it for the purpose of getting the information you may want/need for your higher spiritual purpose. Here is where you can ask all sorts of huge questions that you may have wanted answers to.

Enjoy and I hope you have reached your goal for healing the seven chakras within you.

This is an adventure you can try over and over again and each time you will reach new levels, new places, new visions, so go for it and keep it going! You will never get bored with the process because the process is always changing.

God Bless!

Final Words

I hope you enjoyed this book. It is dedicated to all those looking for a better path and those who want and are willing to do the work to get ahead and be rebalanced in life. I wrote this book to help those who are searching and seeking truth. I love being able to be here for all of you and get these timeless chakra tools out into the universe for all of you to grow.

I am happy you have picked up this book and have chosen this message to come into your home, your life and, last of all, into your energy. We are all here to have complete happiness. I hope this book helped get you closer to that goal and reaching balance within your life.

I have many more books coming, as well as guided meditation CDs, seminars, lectures and retreats. I hope these will keep you looking forward to your own balanced life and spiritual healing.

We are all as One. Whether we see it now or in 100 years from now, we will once again get back to the basics and help reunite each other as one powerful team that will raise this planet's vibration again.

God bless all of you and listen to your angel who is beside you, behind you, or holding you.

Tammy Adams
Master Intuitive Life Coach & Spiritual Healer.

ABOUT THE AUTHOR

Tammy Adams is a Master Intuitive Life Coach & Spiritual Healer. She also goes by the Life Purpose Guru, or you can also simply call her The Shaman. Tammy has been born unveiled for lifetime after lifetime. She has always been born with gifts to communicate with God, the Angels and spirits as well as see, feel, and heal energy and much more. Being born unveiled is a choice she has made lifetime after lifetime before coming to earth so that she can provide guidance, healing, and knowledge of the universe that has been revealed only to the rare few. She is here to help heal our planet, heal the people of our planet, and help everyone discover their life's purpose so that they can then go out into the world and spread the light.

Tammy's life, however, was not always surrounded in light. She was born into a very hostile family environment which was filled with abuse, neglect, and even attempts on her life. Her family did not understand who or what she was and so they condemned her. Even though her upbringing was so harsh, she would not change a thing about her experience. Through that experience, she has learned to connect with the pain and suffering of others to heal and guide them onto their life's path. By choice, she has even lived homeless for 2 years in the San Francisco Bay Area to better understand suffering so that she could find the best possible solution to help those in need.

Her life's path has led her to be mentored by some of the most amazing spiritual leaders of our time. Tammy lived at the Vatican for some time and was mentored by Pope John II as well as Father Phillip during her stay. She then went on to work with Mother

Teresa, His Holiness the Dalai Lama, the Visionaries of Medjugorje, Hopi Indian Shaman and so many others. She has traveled the world over to understand the fullest extent of her gifts and has visited uncharted holy sites which the Angels led her to all in the name of transformation and healing.

Tammy is a non-denominational Spiritual Minister. While traveling in her early years, she studied religions from all different parts of the world. Having direct communication with God, Tammy always knew that God was a part of all people and loves all His children. Her purpose behind studying religions was to learn how people forged their relationship with God so she could connect with them at a higher frequency. Thus, she created the House of Angels Foundation, 501©3. The purpose of the Foundation is to create a space of sanctuary no matter what a person's background. Most importantly, the Foundation's mission is to provide a place of healing, guidance and nurturing for all those in need. If you ask anyone close to Tammy about what kind of person she is, they will all speak to the magnitude of her heart.

You can help support the House of Angels Foundation by donating towards helping them create healing and wellness centers for children and adults in need of food, shelter, healing and love.

Please visit *globehealing.org* to donate.

God Bless!

94404225R00024

Made in the USA
San Bernardino, CA
12 November 2018